the heart of you

A Way to Fly

Reader,

This is a textbook, an instruction manual
for turning your heart into something that
flies and hopes and sings—

Either a bird
or a stone, whistling through the air.

—pleasefindthis

the heart of you

poetry about hope and persistence

iain s. thomas

Dear You,

Here we are at the end of everything.

And when everything else has been taken,
what do we have left but who we are?

All that remains is hope, is goodness,
is sunlight, is the way a name sounds the first
time you hear it, is the human heart, is the
reason we were put here, is the meaning that can
be found only in others, and it's you—because
hope is all of those things and who you are.

And the world needs you. Now more than ever.

—Iain S. Thomas

"How does it start?"

"The book begins

as the poem begins

as living begins:

With light.

With crying as a sign of life."

There is hope hidden in a book, in a song, in a painting, in place, in a sentence, somewhere, written just for you.

I did not forget you.

i did not forget you. i did not forget your
heart. i did not forget your secrets. i did not
forget your truth. i did not forget the things
that make you, you, i did not
forget what was said, i did not forget what was
felt, i am still here, in the space between the
words, in the space between the
sentences—i did not forget you. i did not
forget your heart. i did not forget your
secrets. i did not forget your truth. i did not
forget the things that make you, you, i did not
forget what was said, i did not
forget what was felt, i am still here, in the
space between the words, in the space between
the sentences—i did not forget you. i did
not forget your heart. i did not forget your

What Things Mean

A black cat crossing your path means bad luck.

A bee buzzing near a window means there's something
special in your life you're not seeing.

Standing under mistletoe means someone's going to kiss you.

Ants not walking in a straight line mean it's going to rain.

A butterfly means your dead parents still love you.

Pain in your jaw means you spend too much time in the past.

Not sleeping means you didn't give yourself enough time to think before you got into bed.

Spilling salt means making the devil cry.

A gun means that we're all still monkeys.

Nothing means nothing.

Fire means there's a way to exist beyond what you think is a limit.

Clouds mean you become the sky in the end.

"Do you remember me?"

"I remember you.

We were younger then.

We are older now."

"Do you still hold on?"

"I still hold on.

We held on to each other then.

We can hold on to each other now."

In Comparative Silence

God whispered and said,

I sent you here with so much and
you have only one job: to give it
away, to give it all away until
you're empty, and then
you can come home.

Bloom

One more song,
one more sunset,
one more time
for all
and everything I am
still trying to be.

Here

From pain to light.
From fear to poetry.
From hate to hope.

To There

What a long road from
who you've been
to who you are slowly
becoming.

The First Magic We Learn Is a Word

How big a word "ma" is when you first mumble it
as a child and discover it means
to be held
to be fed
to be warm
to be rocked gently to sleep.
How powerful a word to learn,
a spell that contains all that is good.

Why wouldn't you say it again?

Why wouldn't you want to say it forever?

Journey's End

Child—
I am taking you to your city
and our home is a caravan
and each night we stop
and I try to tell you what the day meant.

One day, we will reach your city,
but our caravan will carry on.

But not before we weep at each day
and what each one meant.

Dandelion Seeds

Gently take out the thorn
the world put in your hand,
blow on where it still hurts,
and turn all your pain
into something that flies
and falls apart,
then creates something new.

1.

Strike light down from heaven.

2.

See the world new in every breath.

3.

Love as only the divine can love.

4.

Forget as only a bird can forget.

Take your truth
place it between the pages
tell your secrets
and catch the light that leaves
your heart.

e lover knows what secrets leave us breathless, heartless,

tless, airless, what do we breathe when we have nothing left to

athe? where do we go when we have nowhere left to go? how do we

back to where we started from? some lover knows what secrets

e us without color, heartless, lightless, airless, what do we

athe when we have nothing left to breathe? where do we go when

have nowhere left to go? how do we get back to where we

ted from? some lover knows what secrets leave us breathless,

tless, lightless, airless, what do we breathe when we have

ing left to breathe? where do we go when we have nowhere left

o? how do we get back to where we started from? some lover knows

t secrets leave us breathless, heartless, lightless, airless, what

e breathe when we have nothing left to breathe? where do we

hen we have nowhere left to go? how do we get back to where we

ted from? some lover knows what secrets leave us breathless,

tless, lightless, airless, what do we breathe when we have

ing left to breathe? where do we go when we have nowhere left

o? how do we get back to where we started from? some lover knows

t secrets leave us breathless, heartless, lightless, airless, what

e breathe when we have nothing left to breathe? where do we

hen we have nowhere left to go? how do we get back to where we

ted from? some lover knows what secrets leave us without color,

tless, lightless, airless, what do we breathe when we have

ing left to breathe? where do we go when we have nowhere left

o? how do we get back to where we started from? some lover knows

t secrets leave us breathless, heartless, lightless, airless, what

e breathe when we have nothing left to breathe? where do we

hen we have nowhere left to go? how do we get back to where we

ted from? some lover knows what secrets leave us breathless,

tless, lightless, airless, what do we breathe when we have

ing left to breathe? where do we go when we have nowhere left

o? how do we get back to where we started from? some lover knows

t secrets leave us breathless, heartless, lightless, airless, what

I love you

—like when a plane dips suddenly.

—Like when everything
is suddenly moving faster
than it's ever moved before.

String on Your Finger

Never forget: You are incredible
in ways you have yet to discover.

You are beautiful in ways that are
impossible for you to see.

There are things strangers love
about you the moment they meet you
that you will never, ever know.

Sleeves

The trick is to make

falling-in-love-with-them

look like

flying-somewhere-your-heart-wants-to-go.

The trick is making

not-knowing-what-you're-doing-with-love

look like

absolutely-knowing-what-you're-doing.

It's just a trick.

A thing to keep up your sleeve.

Making Things Out of Light

Every beautiful thing takes time,
and the time will pass whether you make it
or not.

Look around you:

How many beautiful things might there be
had we all just forgotten about the time?

(So go ahead and make the thing that
changes the world even if it's small.

Even if it's nothing.

There is someone for whom
it will be everything.)

A Word Before You Speak

Tell those who would judge us:

We have walked in the most
sacred spaces and shattered the
windows with the music in our
hearts, letting in all light.

The Lesson

If you can take your anger
and hold it in amber,
you can use it to light the sun.

— Everything you feel is worth something.

How?

Just love like no one taught you how to love,
like love is something new that you just
invented, and then you don't need to say or
write or do anything; then your whole life
becomes a kind of poetry.

(Because I swear, for someone out there, you are
Tony Hawk, Joan of Arc, and Jesus and every
miracle, all rolled into one.)

In Your Marrow

Hold on to goodness,
where all goodness lives,
where sadness and apathy and cynicism
cannot reach, where joy and love
and all the things that make you smile have
been waiting for you to remember them.

(I just want you to know there are no accidents,
that this is all happening the way it was meant
to happen, that you were meant to be here in this
life, being you, reading this, feeling the things
you feel, learning from them and breathing them
in and out into the universe, like a perfect spark
in an eternal, beautiful fire.)

A Hidden Note

Your angel
assigned at birth thinks of you
often,
wonders where you have gone,
what you are doing,
since you hid your head and ducked away from
them, into the shadows.

They know you hurt your heart
and skinned your knees.

The one who watches you has asked me to send you
a message and hide it in this poem:

Come back home.

They Whisper:

Somewhere in your heart,
I keep something like Christmas there.

Fig. 1. Breaking My Heart
Listening to Your Heart Breaking

To Answer Truthfully

When you ask me how I am,

I am everything all the time,

but we are not allowed to say that, so
I say, "I can't complain."

But I can.

I can totally complain.

I could complain for years.

A List

All I want to do is touch every cat gently
behind the ears
And smell every perfume
And linger too long in the wrong places
And love until it hurts to love
And if it's not too late,

everything, everything, everything.

The Other Side of a Blessing

One day you will lose Everything,
and it will be gone, and you will miss
things you did not know you would
miss.

And then Everything will change,
and if you are lucky, you will look
around you and know that there is
a new Everything that one day you
might miss.

And you will taste your food
differently and sip cold water with
the secret joy only someone who has
lost Everything once before knows.

A Poem I Can Only Point To but Cannot Write

Part one is about what made you happy.

Part two is about what made you sad.

Part three is something about sunlight and how it
moves so slowly across the floor.

Me

Me after I make my silly little poems
and gestures at shared experiences
that connect us all on some
fundamental level that lives beyond
words.

Me after I let go of the things
holding me back to embrace the things
pulling me forward.

Me after I love wholly and
completely, like I have never loved
before or will again,
unconditionally, foolishly, without
pain or hesitation.

Me after me.

Just me.

(I do not talk,

and I have spent my life trying to find others

who do not talk

so we can be in each other's company

and not talk about what this feels like.

And not talk about the healing power

of a song without words.

And not talk about the gentleness

that can be found in quiet spaces—

in the sublime joy of the silence before anyone else

wakes up.)

Exercise 1.A

The words became the words
when I stopped trying to write them.

The words became the words
when I started to listen.

Now

After midnight,

we finally gather,

separately, in our own rooms,

the ones who write and paint and make by

small lights in the dark,

and even though the world is quiet,

we know we do not make

the things we make

alone.

Fig. 1.1

A Heart Alive with Defiance and Joy

Walk

It is hard to imagine the rest of the
story, and so we always feel that where we
are right now is the end of the story, that
everything that happened before now got
us here— you forget that once you were far
away. One day, you will go farther still.

With time and patience, you will walk over
mountains as if they were nothing.

Forget Them

You feel bad because you've taken
someone with you—
from when you were young.
And when you're trying to decide
what to do,
you're still asking them,
"Is this right? Is this OK?
Are you happy now?"
And they're not there.
And they cannot answer.
And you will not find peace until you
realize they're gone and you don't need
anyone's permission to be you anymore.

Like a Record

You cannot skip the pain.
Trying to skip it makes it worse.
You must sit with the pain until it
realizes that you are not going
anywhere.
And then the pain gives up.

A Tale

Write the story
that matters,
and let each of your
actions be a word
and each thought
the space between them.

Run

Take what you have to carry now
and put it between us.
I will take what I have to carry
and share it with you.
And the things we carry between us can talk.

And while they talk,
we can get out of here,
we can run, together,
faster than we've ever run before.

Move

With all my body, and all that I am,

I move through the little things

Through the little failures that make me

think it's all for nothing

Through the restless death that stalks us

every minute

Through the smug,

the apathetic, and the cynical,

still

I move.

when all one me...
me what I asked you and if I meant what I said, well
e means is, I don't want to be alone right now, and I don't think you w
sked you and if I meant what I said, well I said what I meant, and I s
don't want to be alone right now, and I don't think you want to be alo
and if I meant what I said, well I said what I meant, and I said what
to be alone right now, and I don't think you want to be alone right n
what I said, well I said what I meant, and I said what I meant, if th
ight now, and I don't think you want to be alone right now either, so
id, well I said what I meant, and I said what I meant, if that's not too
, and I don't think you want to be alone right now either, so maybe w
id what I meant, and I said what I meant, if that's not too confusing,
nk you want to be alone right now either, so maybe we can not be alor
and I said what I meant, if that's not too confusing, to say what one
be alone right now either, so maybe we can not be alone together — Yo
hat I meant, if that's not too confusing, to say what one means, when
ight now either, so maybe we can not be alone together — You asked me
t, if that's not too confusing, to say what one means, when all one me
ther, so maybe we can not be alone together — You asked me what I ask
not too confusing, to say what one means, when all one means is, I do
ybe we can not be alone together — You asked me what I asked you and
sing, to say what one means, when all one means is, I don't want to be
e alone together — You asked me what I asked you and if I meant what
what one means, when all one means is, I don't want to be alone right
ther — You asked me what I asked you and if I meant what I said, well
as, when all one means is, I don't want to be alone right now, and I do
ed me what I asked you and if I meant what I said, well I said what I
means is, I don't want to be alone right now, and I don't think you w
sked you and if I meant what I said, well I said what I meant, and I s
on't want to be alone right now, and I don't think you want to be alor
d if I meant what I said, well I said what I meant, and I said what I
be alone right now, and I don't think you want to be alone right now
l well I said what I meant, and I said what I meant, if that'
lone right now either, so

I meant, if that's not too confu...

t now either, so maybe we can not be alone together – You asked me

if that's not too confusing, to say what one means, when all one mean

r, so maybe we can not be alone together – You asked me what I asked

too confusing, to say what one means, when all one means is, I don't w

e can not be alone together – You asked me what I asked you and if I

ing, to say what one means, when all one means is, I don't want to be

t be alone together – You asked me what I asked you and if I meant wh

what one means, when all one means is, I don't want to be alone right

er – You asked me what I asked you and if I meant what I said, well I

when all one means is, I don't want to be alone right now, and I don't

me what I asked you and if I meant what I said, well I said what I me

means is, I don't want to be alone right now, and I don't think you w

asked you and if I meant what I said, well I said what I meant, and I

I don't want to be alone right now, and I don't think you want to be al

nd if I meant what I said, well I said what I meant, and I said what I

to be alone right now, and I don't think you want to be alone right

nt what I said, well I said what I meant, and I said what I meant, if

right now, and I don't think you want to be alone right now either, so

well I said what I meant, and I said what I meant, if that's not too co

I don't think you want to be alone right now either, so maybe we can

what I meant, and I said what I meant, if that's not too confusing, to

k you want to be alone right now either, so maybe we can not be alone

nd I said what I meant, if that's not too confusing, to say what one m

e alone right now either, so maybe we can not be alone together – You

t I meant, if that's not too confusing, to say what one means, when al

now either, so maybe we can not be alone together – You asked me wha

f that's not too confusing, to say what one means, when all one means

so maybe we can not be alone together – You asked me what I asked yo

o confusing, to say what one means, when all one means is, I don't wa

e can not be alone together – You asked me what I asked you and if I

to say what one means, when all one means is, I don't want to be alo

To Do

What was not meant to be
will not be.

This does not mean do easy things
or hard things.

It just means be brave and choose
what should be done.

The little things we choose to do
change our lives.

Reasons to Fall in Love with Life

The way a cat sits on you.
The way milk flows through cold coffee.
The way it rains in summer.
The feeling of ink sinking
into plain white paper.

To Pray

It's in our bodies, to think
of the sky or the sun or
someone who died a long
time ago, and all we can do
is try and
remember that we can
choose what praying looks
like for us.

Maybe God is
a stranger.

Maybe kindness and love
are all that matter.

In This Moment

Look around,
beyond the metaphors
and the signs and what could be signs,
and try to see what is, not what it means,
just what is.

Exercise 2

The right thing heals you;
the wrong thing hurts.

(Healing can hurt,
but hurting can never heal.)

Sunburn

I once gently touched the sun
and felt what ten thousand summers
feel like all at once.

It happened when I was with you.

When your hand
gently brushed against mine.

(Their body softly next to yours in a car, on a
bus, on a train, traveling somewhere you always
meant to be, to eat something sweet and share it
with each other, turning to each other at the
same time, glancing at each other, and ebbing and
flowing, toward and away as you experience the
purpose of everything—to share space and time,
in the little time and space you are given.)

A Mechanical Heart

They gave the computer a heart and
trained it on many hearts, then they
made it watch every movie and read
every book, then they made it hold
hands for ten hours every day with
someone who lost someone, and then
on the day they woke it up, all it
could say was

"Oh no. Oh no, no, no, no."

It covered the whole screen.

Feature List

An app that just saves every picture to a folder named
"For you after I die."

An app that turns your good intentions into actions and
explains everyone else's intentions in a way you can
understand.

An app that asks you to write poems and make art
for robots.

An app that makes your plane as late as you are.

An app that tells you when someone is missing you.

This Too

There is a mouse
somewhere in winter
cold in some forgotten hole
in some forgotten field
looking around and thinking
with its last thought:
This could be beautiful too.

An End

Don't worry about the end of your life
your life will end
in whatever way it is meant to—
worry only about spending too much time
thinking about it.
Worry only
when worrying will solve something,
which is very, very rare indeed.

To Stay

The most important moments of your
life are all around you—not before,
not after, just now.

Come back.

You Are

Everything is only what it
needs to be,
and you don't have to be
anyone but who you are.

Burn

People share the brave poems,
the ones that make them
think that even in spite of
this, of all this fire and
brimstone and ash and pain,
that it is worth staying,
because it is,
because in the end, that's
what all poetry is:

the choice to stay in a
moment that is on fire.

Encompassed

I have seen the best of you pick up
pain,
and hold it, and say,

"You are also part of me,
and so I will love you too."

Just Not Me

Somewhere there is someone who knows how to
fall in love easier than this, slower than
this, gentler than this, but it is not me.

One Photograph Every Day

Just notice things, things
you don't see
— and take one photo
every day of something
boring, something mundane
and not worth noticing; keep
them, make a treasure chest of
things that'll one day make
you cry in case, one day, you
really need to cry.

Write Down What Matters:

No one asked me if it's my birthday,
and it's my birthday.

My daughter bought a thing with the word "Dad"
stamped on it, and I cried.

Grass grew through the bricks outside.

In the greatest scheme of things,
everything is quiet.

Fig. 2. Moving Away from the Things
That Matter to the Detriment of
All That I Am
in the Damning Light of Forever

Facing Seat

There are two people on a train
sitting across from each other,
and they're both listening to
the same song.

The same book kept them up
last night, and the same thing
is killing them, and the same
thing, if they find each other,
can bring them back to life.

(Let us take turns dying

until it doesn't matter

and we lose interest.

Let's take turns ending the world

and not calling

and forgetting who we are

until it means nothing.

Until nothing hurts anymore.)

It's Nothing

If everything feels important,
then doing nothing—
just taking a breath,
just for a little while—
is just as important as everything else.

Maybe

Maybe hell is just living
while denying yourself the
simple things that
would make you happy—
because someone once
convinced you that you
didn't deserve them.

There You Are

Only for the ones who feel too much,
they are all
that I have lost
—where have you been,
I have so much to tell you.

To Light

Children, like plants,
grow toward light.
Whether on a screen, in
a heart or the
sunlight outside, or
in a book, they grow to
fill their containers,
and then, if we do a
good job, they
overflow them.

Not Alone

You don't ever have
to feel lonely;
how you feel
is how anyone

feels

somewhere.

What It Means

It means twisting and turning, from one thing to
another, from death to life, from spring to
autumn, from the start to the end, again and again.

It means collecting things and keeping the ones
that mean something and being brave enough to let
go of the ones that don't anymore.

It means your heart breaking and growing, breaking
and growing, breaking and growing because love is a
tide, it's a dawn, it's a bird returning home, it's the
start and the end of a rosary.

It means being as close as you can to the ones you
love and—

in truth, I cannot tell you what it means.

I can only tell you what it means to me.

Forgetting This

It can be hard to remember, but
we get to choose who we are in
some fundamental way that the
world has a habit of
making us forget—I'm not
saying that we get to choose to
be successful or talented, but
we get to choose how we see
ourselves and who we want to be
and what we want to do while
we're here, living the brief
life we've been given. Even if
it's in small, quiet moments,
even if it's not our full-time
job, even if it's not everything
we wanted it to be, we still get
to choose a little.

Start Here

It's not impossible, but it's harder to make mistakes when you start with love.

Not trying to do the right thing or the fair thing or the caring thing—all these things come after you make the decision to start with love.

It won't always be right, and it's not foolproof, but love is a better place to start than anywhere else.

Radiate

Everything can be beautiful
when you make yourself a part of it—
join all of us on the other side
of what is mine and what is yours,
because all of us
are just parts of each other.

"We've all agreed we're the same person."

"What do you mean?"

"We think it came from one initial
conversation in which we turned to
ourselves and said,

'I think you're me. Am I you? You feel like
me in different skin.'

And then it became a series of
agreements between individuals who felt
like they were the same, just in
different skin; we became something
bigger than ourselves, a divine
connection, and we promised to
never bomb ourselves or brutalize ourselves
or hurt ourselves ever again."

The One Truth of All Things

Outside, you see them sit on a park
bench, the emptiness of the world,
and they take out a letter, and they
read it, and they touch their face,
and they turn it over, and they
touch their face again, and there, in
whatever secrets that letter holds,
lives the truth we're all trying to
tell.

Ripple

To trace the moments across
your skin like stones
across water—this one,

                    this one,

this one.

It Will

This will end you, it will destroy
you in ways you cannot imagine,
it will destroy you until there is
nothing left of you—and then the
miracle will begin—you will come
back from nothing, you will make
yourself whole, and you will heal,
and you will overcome the thing
that absolutely destroyed and
ended you.

No Warning

Do not worry about any fire.

You will burn hotter and longer than
every fire.

Even Here

Even in decay,
flowers bloom and one thing
becomes another, and we change,
and change again, we become,
we become, we were light and
soil, now we're this, and we will
become everything again.

Now This

This is who you are,
not loud, not quiet,
just someone becoming
themselves with every breath.

Explorers and Lovers

Beneath the ocean lives
another world of
shipwrecks and monsters
and secrets,
and I feel like sometimes
your skin is an ocean too.

Judas

I was who I was,
now I have
become who I am,
and who I was lives
somewhere else
and writes lies to me about how
good we had it and tries to make
me forget who I am.

Out of Everything

I hope this email doesn't find you.

I hope you are far away from your email.

I hope email is the last thing you're
thinking of.

And if it does find you, I hope this
email finds you mad, mad, mad, running
through the streets, aching and human,
arching your back at the moon, desperate
for wonder, plucking flowers from hidden
gardens, falling over yourself to become
something new.

Silver Sparkling Signage

Just point toward the thing you
want to be every day
and follow the direction you're
pointing.
You don't have to be fast.
You just have to remember.

Find Your Way

Somewhere inside,
I know the rain has stopped and
something new is outside,
waiting to be discovered,
in wet grass.
On shiny pavements.

A Home

This is the poem
And it
has four
walls and a roof
Because a poem can be comfortable—
A place to come back to
when everywhere else turns you away.

Who I've Become

A heart,
behind a mask,
behind a heart,
behind a mask,
behind a heart,
behind a poem.

The Price of Everything

Even though you are sad, it does
not mean you made a mistake.

It just means that when you
choose something better for
yourself, the cost of doing that
is being sad for a while.

In This Place

In the heart of every great,
old city,
there is a space where
someone fell in love with the
water and the soil
and just went
"Here."

No More Fear

Change is only as painful as your
resistance to that change.
When we let go of what it is,
we open ourselves up to what could be.

Sparkling Toward the End

There have been no great exhibitions of paintbrushes,
or life-changing concerts remembered for
the quality of the sound system.

I have yet to see a pen as moving or profound as the
words it might write, or a camera as beautiful as my
favorite films.

Fig. 3

"What are you waiting for?"

"Just forever."

A Highway Out of Your Heart

Any full life is one that is filled sometimes with great
beauty and sometimes with pain.
So yes, you hurt, but if that isn't a sign
of something bigger for you,
then I don't know what is.

— When we got lost coming back from that
stupid club and
— Yeah and
— How we had to ask the only person we could
find, that guy waiting for the bus
— And how
— He couldn't speak English and you had to act
out
— How I had to act out
— What finding your way home looked like
— And I made a pyramid with my hands to be a
roof
— And I pretended like I was a door
— And we were mad, we were mad
— And he knew we were mad, and it didn't
matter.

We Know

We all know deep down what
we have to do. We hide from it,
but late at night, the voice
speaks, quietly,

"You will not be free until
you hear me."

Meaningfully Here

We do not see ourselves when we
look out at the world; we see only
others, and so we need to
remember that we are a part of
the world and everything in it,
connected to it fundamentally, in
ways we must call to mind,
and heart, again and again.

Light Fall

I try to take the
shining in my heart
to someone else's,
to take what shines
in me and shines on me,
and share what light
I can in the
space between us.

Even Then

Do not worry; wherever you go,
my light and my heart go with you,
my love travels by your side endlessly,
even into the darkest dark,
even into the end.

Close Them

If you feel like you've been
here before, like you've been
traveling in circles, ask
yourself what
signpost you're not seeing,
what lesson
you're not learning.

The road changes when you
close your eyes.

Candle Burn

And I may never live long enough to
see your wedding, if you ever feel like
getting married, so all I can hope is
that I love you enough right now
to make you feel like I'm there.

Even if I'm somewhere else.

Even if I'm just the light in the room.

What I Believe

You asked and I'm sorry I Ummed and Aahed. This is what I believe:

I believe in God, Superman, Krishna, and the ever-living love that flows through all people, objects, things, and ideas. I believe we are an expression of this love, a way for this love to know itself in a million different ways. I believe love requires complexity for it to reach its fullest form, and that is why sometimes we cut our fingers on tin cans, or people we love tell us they don't love us—these are not bad things; they are notes, layers, textures that create tension between all the other notes and layers—I am not telling you to be sad; I am telling you that being sad is a part of everything and you should embrace feeling sad when you feel it, because once you have felt it, you can let it go, you can breathe it out like a breeze through a hot day.

I believe we are together after we die. I believe the feeling you have when we are together now is an echo of how we spent eternity before you got here and what eternity will be like when we both leave (me long before you, hopefully; this life is important, and I hope you get to experience every part of it).

I believe we should pray and that the way we pray is being kind to each other, by knowing our neighbors and by being true to who we are and pursuing what lies deepest in our hearts.

The greatest challenge of your life will be to accept yourself as being worthy of the things you want. You are.

You are everything you need to be to pursue your greatest calling, your highest purpose, your greatest possible achievement. What that is will change from moment to moment. Sometimes it will mean pushing with all your strength. Sometimes it will mean gently holding yourself and expecting nothing more than what already is.

I am sorry I cannot give you a shorter or simpler answer, but this is what I believe.

Remember:

Maybe you're not depressed.

Maybe it's all just a bit shit.

Maybe

Maybe your best was needed somewhere else.

Put your best where it matters.

Give your best to what deserves it.

Stay

And in this life you were told you
could do anything and you did not have
to follow a path beyond the one your
heart called out for—and the only
pain there really is, is the pain of
walking away from your heart.

Run from Heaven

You cannot keep your heart safe forever;
at some point, you must let it run free
into whatever fields it seeks,
whether those fields are filled
with heather or thorns.
Your heart wants what it wants,
and if you starve it,
if you try and trap it in your chest,
it will in desperation fall in love
with the shadows it sees on the wall
and think that sadness is a kind of heaven.

The Difference

The truth hides from us behind our
thinking—our thinking gets in the way of
what we know—because knowing and
thinking are two different things.
We think about politics.
We know our neighbors.

Gentle Water

You are out on dry land, and you do
not feel the water of everything
that matters lapping against your
skin—you are lying on a beach
somewhere at the edge of the
universe, dreaming all of this—
but if you can be still enough and
quiet enough, you can wake up and
feel the soft sun on the parts of you
that are infinite.

Fig. 4

The Small Things We Find Life in That
Save Us on an Almost Daily Basis

Just This

You just have to do what you can.
Don't worry about the rest.
It takes care of itself.
Take care of you.

Exercise 1.B

No one teaches you the grammar;
you just catch yourself
keeping track of what the voice
in the dark says:

(Write down your heart, it's worth
writing down.)

(Writing it down might be a way
to get better.)

Cantrip

Whatever hurt you in the dark,
I take away with light.
Whatever hurt you in the night,
I take away with the dawn.
I whisper the prayer, the magic
spell, the song that takes it away
and leaves you clean and
together.

Endless

There is no poetry, just the way rain
falls at a certain angle on a window.
There is no poetry, just yearning for
winter in summer and yearning for
summer in winter.
There is no poetry, just this.
Just the great confession.
Just the great apology.
You just call it poetry because you need
a name for something that isn't the news
or an invoice or a recipe.
But it's just everything that doesn't have
a name.

(Thank you for your eternal promise;
I give you mine in return.
(God keeps our promises and our oaths
in a pocket. He holds them tight.))

(I did not know how people died
when I was younger,
but now I think I know; I think
the idea of letting go has
become so much easier.
There are so many days when I
would be happy to let go
even though, in the end, I know
I'll want to stay just a little bit
longer with you.)

The Workday

I have to work, to write down my heart, so
that means I need to be distracted,
I need to go and find something that
breaks it, something that destroys me,
that no one else can see.

I need to clock in, so I need to go and
stare at a cloud until it turns into
something that reminds me of something
I thought I'd forgotten forever, I've got
to do my time sheets and fill in all the
times, I stopped in the middle of a shop
and stared at a fridge for no reason
other than the ice cream reminded me of
my mother's eyes.

I need to get there on time, to the first
leaf that falls, guys, please, Dad's busy
—he's trying to make sense of the things
that don't make sense, he's writing them
down in his own special way, he's breaking
and fixing the things that don't need to
be broken or fixed, he's taking and giving
his heart away to everything that
reflects light, he's on a call, with God,
be quiet.

Unspoken

We do not talk about it,
but I am so different,
and you are so different too,
and maybe that's why I'm here
writing this and you're here
reading it.

Enough

All I can do
is think of you,
because thinking
is a kind of magic
that we can all do.

Traveling

One day you will get here,
and then you will want to go
somewhere else
—and don't let anyone make you
feel bad about that,
don't even worry about it—
that's how moving works.

Breaking Falls

We saw you jump
because you thought that
you would fall faster than
your breaking heart could
keep up.

Just so you know,
when you reached the
ground,
it caught up to all of us.

The Litany of Impossible Things

Impossible things don't have to be sad,
you can do them anyway,
you can grab your friends and say,

"Hey, guess what, sucker—we're doing
impossible things today."

And then you can bring your dead
friends back to life,
and do the things you can't do anymore,
and fall in love with the people you're
not allowed to fall in love with
anymore.

Entry Fee

To be an artist,
just be kinda messed up in
your own special way
and vaguely coherent,
and the second part is
entirely optional.

Desolate

In the book, the boy swings the sling
around his head and releases the
stone, and it strikes the giant in the
head and kills him, but in this room,
it's just the battlefield and me and
the giant of the things
between us, and there is nothing left
to kill here anymore.

Growing

Where will we find our friends, and
what will they look like when we find
them?

In the dark, they will remind us of the
best parts of us.

They will be the greatest gifts we
could give each other.

A Passing Thought

When you think of me after I'm gone,
that is me touching your arm
and wanting you to know
that everything is OK
and that I still believe
we are together in the end.

Cold Oceans

Wade in.

Do not go lightly or slowly.

The cold will scare you.

Embrace it, all at once.

Revelations

Can't you see, it's the end
of the world, and I stubbed
my toe, and I can't pay the
mortgage, and what will we
do?

(When the world ends,
I will stand at the end with
you, homeless, with stubbed
toes.)

Receipts

Outside your house, and the car won't start,
and your dad is at the door, mad as hell
— we'll get out of here one day, I swear.

Walking home in the starlight, smoking
stolen cigarettes
— we'll get out of here one day, I swear.

A meeting with the pastor and your mother,
I'll tell you again, if I ever get the chance
— we'll get out of here one day, I swear.

And now, so many years away from there,
if you still read what I write:

I told you.
I told you.
I told you.

Requests

Open your heart to feelings, even the
ones you've told yourself you're not
allowed to feel.

Anyone

Be the one someone needs when they
think they don't need anyone.

Back for the Wounded

It's OK.

You've got more than you think.
It just feels like less right now, in this
moment, in this space.
You can stand on the edge;
I'll stand with you.
We'll come back down together
when you're ready to come back down.

Even Now

Even in forever, there is time left
for waiting.

Even in forever, there is a way to
pull yourself together.

I Loved Too Much

Too much for lovers.
Too much for sinners and saints.
Too much for me.
Never enough for you.

What If?

What if we kissed in the poem?
Not at the start; that would be too much.
We could tease each other in the middle of
it, lean too close to each other,
reach past you as if all I wanted to do was
get something out of the drawer.
Toward the end, you could pretend you found
something on my face and you needed to take
a closer look,
and in the end, here, we could kiss and feel
the soda bubbles in our chests.

Go

Our love is a place that we can go.
It is a planet we can discover together.
Perhaps without air or hope of return.
But I would still hold your hand and ask
you to go to space with me.

Walk Often

There was no path to my heart until you
walked the soft grass, turning it beneath
your heel.

Becoming

Everything becomes part of you
eventually. The road out the window as
you drive. The soft fall sunsets.
The feeling of your skin touching
someone else's.

You do these things, and then one day you
become them.

To Live and Die

I could have lived and died anywhere,
but here I am, living and dying with you.

And what better way to live?

And what better way to die?

Memo

Inadvertently, I
have fallen in love.
Inadvertently, I have
given you
everything I am, and
now I cannot separate
you from me.

Inadvertently, I
must ask you to never
leave.

Inadvertently, I
ask you to give
enough of me back,
just to be here
with you.

Soft Notes

Where is love born? Here?

— when I kiss the tips of your fingers.

— when you rest your head against me.

— when your hand reaches for mine, as mine
reaches for yours.

Leave Me Behind

Words as pull-ups.
As jumping jacks for the heart.
As miles. As stretches.
Poems as medicine.
As bitter.
As a way to find something better
on the other side.
Poems as a ritual.
As tea.
As communion.
This is blood. This is a body.
As a poem.

What Hope Is

Hope is not where you're going; it is the
thing that gets you to where you're going.

It is the burning car that takes you
through the flames.

Dark Rules

I think, for some people,
somewhere in their manual, it
says there needs to be a rule, not
anything specific, just a rule:
You cannot stay up past ten, you
cannot write with
anything except a hotel ballpoint
pen, you can think only when you
are in the shower, you can love
someone only when they don't love
you back.

Painted Heart

A heart painted
with silver and gold.
A heart painted
with all the colors in your eyes.
A heart painted
with everything we forget.
A heart painted
with running makeup.
A heart painted
with what we were.
A heart painted
with every future that branched
from this one.

Remember

Go and find the song in
nature that hides
beneath the leaves—
remember that it's there.
Find the secret woven into
the grass. Find something
made just for you, hidden
between the streetlights
and the stars.

Starshine

Some distilleries let you make your own
blend of whiskey and, my God, I made
moonshine and that upset everyone, and
that's everything I've ever done: give me
the active ingredient, the thing that
makes the thing the thing, and let it be
the truest version of itself it can be.

In the Future

One day, I will apologize for not being
perfect, because perfect is what you deserve,
and all I've ever managed was my best, and even
that, at times, was my worst.

To Write

Just use the pen that works—
whatever that pen looks like,
if the pen looks like walking
alone, then walk alone.
If the pen looks like sitting
with a cat, then sit with the cat.
If the pen looks like music,
then move, and the pen will
write.

Kind

Don't try and be clever.
Try and be kind. Cleverness and pride
have hurt more people than anything
else.

Cleverness is just cruelty
wearing different clothes.
Kindness is so much more.

Take Time

Learn the lessons
taught by hard hands
and soft hearts.

All of It

I like to think
that everything is possible.

That there is a world where it's just
you and me and the moment we meet.

As every moment.

As everything.

Static

You don't see the hope dripping
down your skin because you have
lost your sweet tooth.
There is joy, if you have the
patience to find it. Listen to the
music on the radio in the next
room:
Doesn't that sound like hope?

Catch and Release

Here, said the universe, here you are.
Here is everything you could be,
here is a moon, and a highway,
and a river, and a song on the radio.

Swirl It in Your Mouth

Don't hope before the end, when hope is
the last thing left.
Keep it. Pretend you don't hope.
Save it for the very end.
A last match in the darkness,
to light a forest fire.

Death Is No Good

Some died quick and some died slow and
some died somewhere
between those points, but none have died
what you might call good deaths
—there are no good deaths—
and the only good thing about death
is the life you live before it.

(I built a kingdom
in the place you go
when you close your eyes in the
dentist's chair.)

Days as Math

There are days that act as dividing
lines in every life,
points before and after,
and sometimes they are so distinct,
you can feel yourself crossing them.

Why Write

Write not to placate, not to assure;
write to set ablaze, to ignite what soft wool
and tinder lie hidden beneath the skin
of all of us.

Write to shoot arrows at what keeps you from
walking outside at night, into the softly
glooming dark.

Write to punch the fascism of apathy in
its stupid face.

The Steps

The keyboard as a bow, to shoot
an arrow at a heart, at the vein
in the arm.

The keyboard as a steering wheel,
as a thing to take you somewhere,
as a way out of here.

The keyboard as steps, as a way
to dance with the dead.

ot where I went to sleep - I am five years old and being carried in a soft blanket by my mother, having falle

to stay asleep so she'll carry me a little longer - I am nine years old and lying upside down on the back sea

entle beat of the streetlights appearing again and again hums me back somewhere special, while the stars sta

nd I am fourteen years old and sleeping on the floor of the YMCA because that's where you still are, poking t

essed with an album that I'll never know or hear again but whose music haunts me still - I wake up and I am n

anced an ashtray on my head - God fucking damnit - I am twenty-three and waking up to a phone call from my

at I'm OK, and please tell Dad I love him and I miss you too and I'll be home soon - I wake up and I've dozed o

r my son to wake up, sleeping with a bush of electrodes on his head - I wake up and I am reading my diary di

and this is a job, and this is a job, and this is a job - and I wake up, one day God almighty, I swear I will w

I don't know if I'm the same person anymore but I keep on waking up, not where I went to sleep - I am five yea

oft blanket by my mother, having fallen asleep in the car, pretending to stay asleep so she'll carry me a lit

d lying upside down on the back seat so the sky is at my feet and the gentle beat of the streetlights appeari

somewhere special, while the stars stay still and silent - I wake up and I am fourteen years old and sleeping

that's where you still are, poking tattoos with broken pens and obsessed with an album that I'll never know c

ts me still - I wake up and I am nineteen in a bar and someone balanced an ashtray on my head - God fuckin

king up to a phone call from my mother and I'm promising her that I'm OK and please tell Dad I love him and

- I wake up and I've dozed off in the hospital, waiting for my son to wake up, sleeping with a bush of elect

I am reading my diary disguised as poetry to strangers and this is a job, and this is a job, and this is a jo

ghty, I swear I will wake up and I will be home - and I don't know if I'm the same person anymore but I keep

sleep - I am five years old and being carried in a soft blanket by my mother, having fallen asleep in the car

n that I'll never know or hear again but whose music haunts me still – I wake up and I am nineteen in a bar a

n my head – God fucking damnit – I am twenty-three and waking up to a phone call from my mother and I'm pr

tell Dad I love him and I miss you too and come home soon – I wake up and I've dozed off in the hospital, w

eping with a bush of electrodes on his head – I wake up and I am reading my diary disguised as poetry to str

is a job, and this is a job – and I wake up, one day – God Almighty, I swear I will wake up and I will be home

ame person anymore but I keep on waking up, not where I went to sleep – I am five years old and being carrie

having fallen asleep in the car, pretending to stay asleep so she'll carry me a little longer – I am nine yea

the back seat so the sky is at my feet and the gentle beat of the streetlights appearing again and again hums

le the stars stay still and silent – I wake up and I am fourteen years old and sleeping on the floor of the Y

are, poking tattoos with broken pens and obsessed with an album that I'll never know or hear again but whos

ke up and I am nineteen in a bar and someone balanced an ashtray on my head – God fucking damnit – I am tw

ne call from my mother and I'm promising her that I'm OK and please tell Dad I love him and I miss you too a

and I've dozed off in the hospital, waiting for my son to wake up, sleeping with a bush of electrodes on his h

y diary disguised as poetry to strangers and this is a job, and this is a job, and this is a job – and I wake u

I will wake up and I will be home – and I don't know if I'm the same person anymore but I keep on waking up

ve years old and being carried in a soft blanket by my mother, having fallen asleep in the car, pretending t

ittle longer – I am nine years old and lying upside down on the back seat so the sky is at my feet and the gen

ring again and again hums me back somewhere special, while the stars stay still and silent – I wake up and I

eping on the floor of the YMCA because that's where you still are, poking tattoos with broken pens and obsess

know or hear again but whose music haunts me still – I wake up and I am nineteen in a bar and someone balan

An End

You don't need to say anything.
We're already here.
We're already doing this.
What more can we say?
What more can we do?

To Learn

There is no virtue in heartbreak.

But there are always lessons.

Wave Goodbye

And each night, I held that sip
from the last bottle in my mouth
for a minute or more, until it
turned into soft amber.
And I swallowed the sweet,
sugary darkness.

No World at All

How could I not cry, holding you, saying,
"I missed you, I missed you, I missed you."

Show me what world that doesn't happen in.

Unconventional daily acts of love:

Reading the book you recommended.

Waiting for you to catch up.

Gently thinking of you and hoping
that you're thinking of me.

Sharing this universe.

(Do you know how hard it is to name a poem?

Pin it down, the butterfly that flew out of your mouth,
and then give it a name.

This one is a star. This one is a hand held.
This one is God's heart.

This one is the first light.

This one is gentleness.

This one is a burst of static on the TV.

This one is the day you discovered music could talk to
you.

This one is everyone you've ever loved.

This one is a paper plane on fire.)

What We Carry

You don't have to carry tomorrow.

You can let go of yesterday.

Today is all you need to hold.

To Be a Fish

They sometimes find fish on the ground
after forest fires, from where the
helicopters dropped the water from lakes.
It must be something to leave your world
and discover the sky, and see the horizon,
and know that there are things far more
incredible than you ever dreamed. Maybe
there are many lakes. Maybe we're all just
fish who've forgotten about the sky.

All There Is

All I see is someone holding the seconds
and moments and minutes that make my
heart beat.

All I see is endless.

All I see is everything.

All I see is you.

Go Now

But only if you can forget me.

Only if you can promise you'll never think
of what could've been.

Only if you can live with yourself every
day after this one.

And if you can, then by all means:
Go.

Don't

Child, don't aspire to us;
we all wish we were you and knew the things you knew,
with all the fullness of your heart,
with all the infinite strength in your bones.

The Dark Isn't the Problem

We come from the dark, and to the dark we will return.

If you close your eyes,
in many ways
you are going home.

"And now?"

"Now we close our eyes, and we go home."

The Heart of You: Poetry About Hope and Persistence
copyright © 2025 by Iain S. Thomas. All rights reserved.
Printed in China. No part of this book may be used or reproduced
in any manner whatsoever without written permission except in
the case of reprints in the context of reviews.

Andrews McMeel Publishing
a division of Andrews McMeel Universal
1130 Walnut Street, Kansas City, Missouri 64106

www.andrewsmcmeel.com

25 26 27 28 29 TEN 10 9 8 7 6 5 4 3 2 1

ISBN: 978-1-5248-9380-4

Library of Congress Control Number: 2024950753

Editor: Melissa Zahorsky
Art Director: Holly Swayne
Production Editor: Kayla Overbey
Production Manager: Julie Skalla

Andrews McMeel Publishing is committed to the responsible use of natural
resources and is dedicated to understanding, measuring, and reducing the
impact of our products on the natural world. By choosing this product, you
are supporting responsible management of the world's forests. The FSC® label
means that the materials used for this product come from well-managed
FSC®-certified forests, recycled materials, and other controlled sources.

ATTENTION: SCHOOLS AND BUSINESSES
Andrews McMeel books are available at quantity discounts with bulk
purchase for educational, business, or sales promotional use. For information,
please e-mail the Andrews McMeel Publishing Special Sales Department:
sales@andrewsmcmeel.com.

Enjoy *The Heart of You* as an audiobook, wherever audiobooks are sold.

Explore the Souls Trilogy

Available wherever books are sold.